MW00715716

Healing-from-hurt
Therapy

Healing-from-hurt Therapy

written by
Lisa O. Engelhardt

illustrated by
R.W. Alley

ABBEY PRESS

Publications
St. Meinrad, IN 47577

Text © 2016 by Lisa O. Engelhardt
Illustrations © 2016 by Saint Meinrad Archabbey
Published by Abbey Press Publications
St. Meinrad, Indiana 47577

Library of Congress Control Number
2016950921

ISBN 978-0-87029-712-0

Printed in the United States of America.

Foreword

This is a book I never wanted to write and you probably never wanted to read. But here we are. We have each suffered some heartrending hurt, which can come in many guises: a tragic loss, ruined relationship, personal betrayal, physical or emotional abuse, shattered dream—to name just a few.

Feeling hurt is not a happy place to be. The heartache can become an unwanted daily companion that consumes our life. It can grow into obsessive thoughts of bitterness or revenge. It can threaten our physical wellbeing. It may seem like it's always been there and will never end, dousing any hope for happiness.

Although we may feel that we'll never get past this, it is possible to find our way back home to our true self. It begins with holding our hearts open to God's goodness and grows with the help of healing resources. It endures through a daily attitude of forgiveness. In the end, we find that easing our anguish comes not from hiding or abiding it, but from rekindling our love for God, ourselves, and others—even those who grievously hurt us.

Time by itself doesn't heal all wounds. But through courage and faith, we can get back on the path to wholeness and wellness. May this book be a worthy guide.

1.

Life can deal some terrible blows. You may have experienced a deep loss, a profound betrayal, a broken relationship, a serious illness or disability, a family crisis, or a shattered dream.

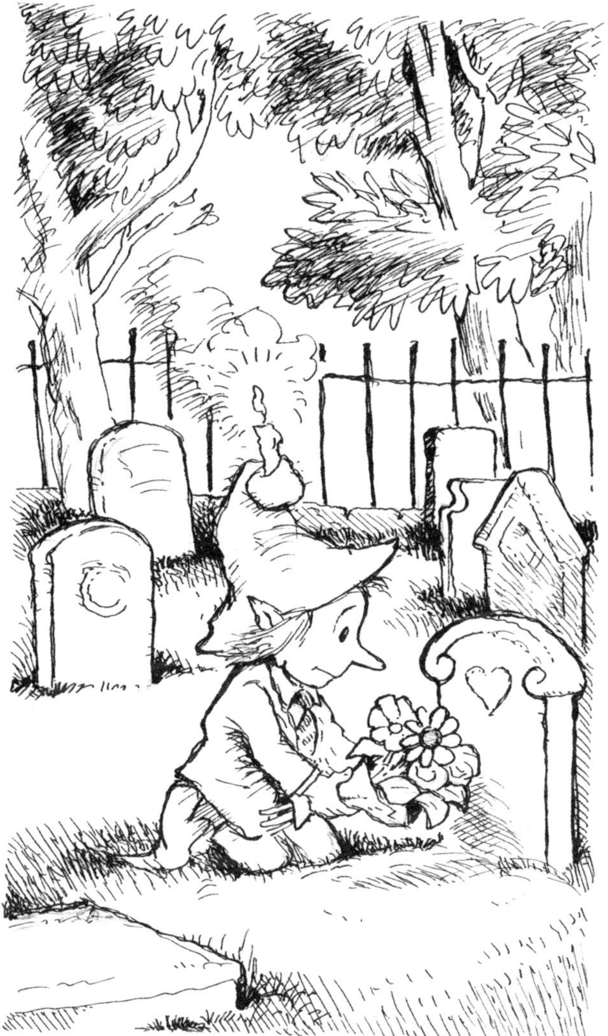

2.

Some hurts are big, long-lasting, and life-changing. Some are more minor, but still annoying and persistent. Some continue to victimize us long after the initial blow.

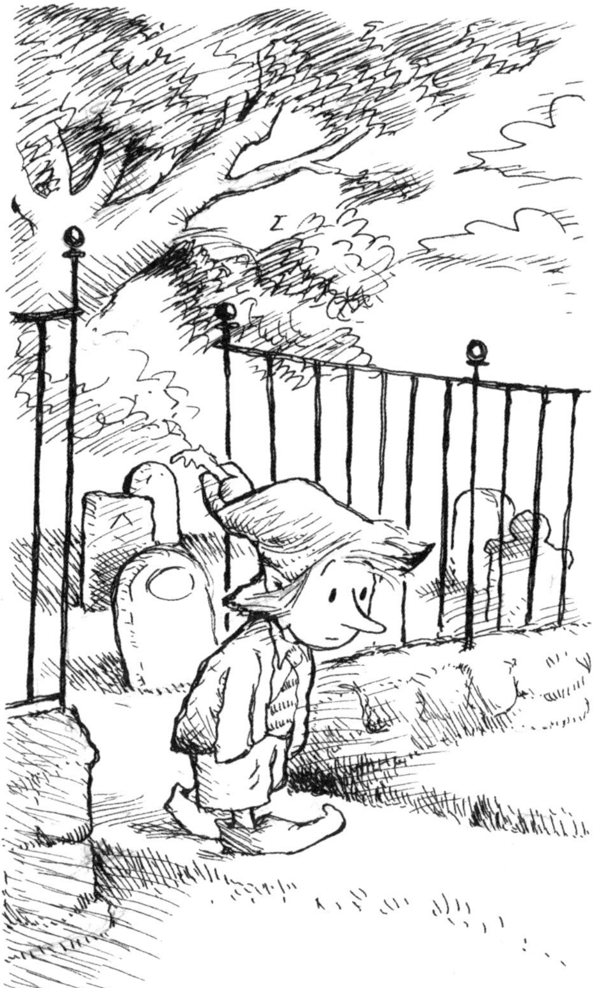

3.

Deep hurt can evoke intense emotions: anger, sadness, blame, shame, helplessness. Hurt gone "underground" can become anxiety or depression.

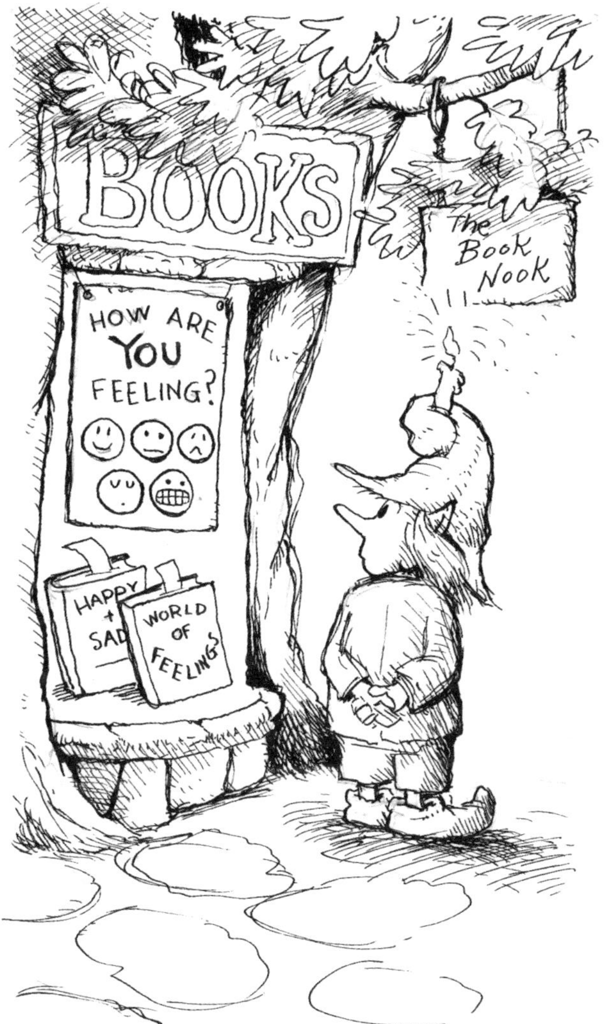
BOOKS
The Book Nook
HOW ARE YOU FEELING?
HAPPY + SAD
WORLD OF FEELINGS

4.

Don't let yourself be defined by brokenness. Yes, a very bad thing happened. But you are bigger and stronger than this hurt.

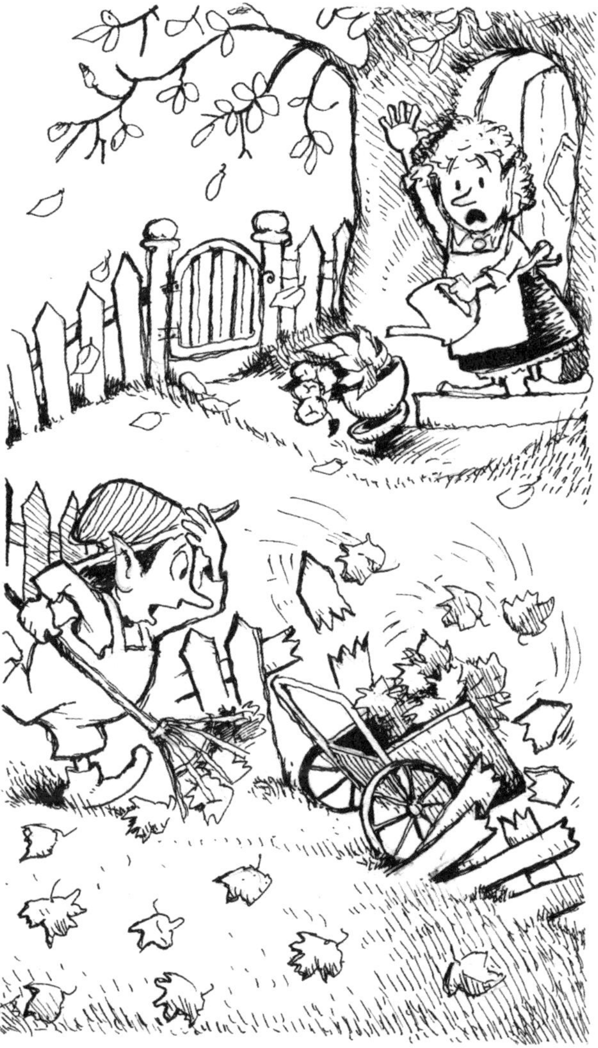

5.

You are not responsible for the damage that life or others have done to you. You are responsible for how you go forth from this moment. Reclaim your wellbeing.

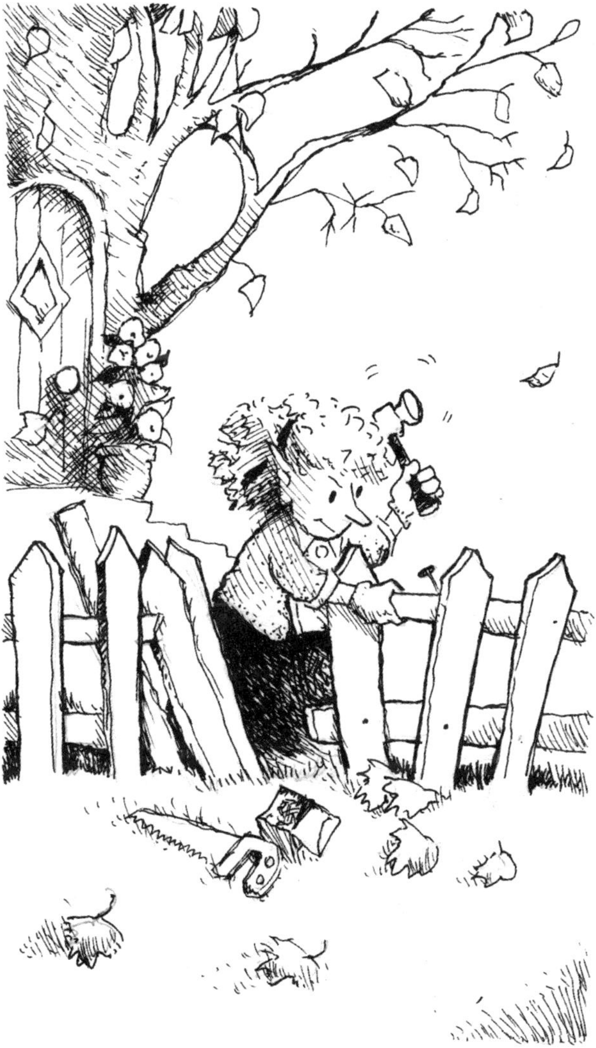

6.

It's natural to want to protect
ourselves from more injury.
We may put on an "armor" of
self-reliance and control. But
this can shield us from the help
of God and others. Be open to
the support available to you.

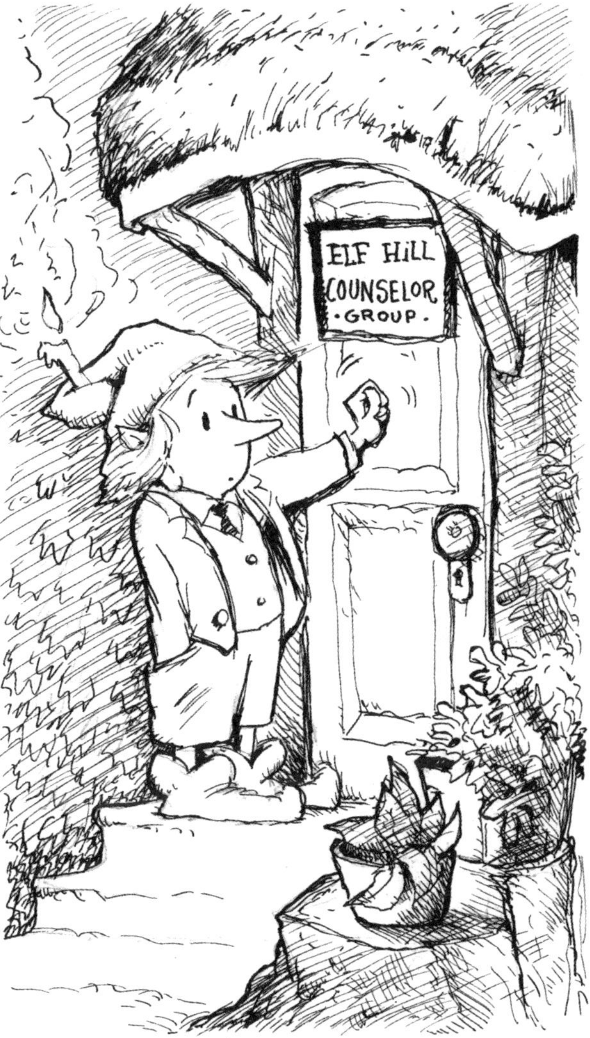
ELF HILL
COUNSELOR
·GROUP·

7.

You may need to revisit the original injury in order to heal it. Summon the courage to re-experience the injury you suffered, so that you can move on to healing and wholeness.

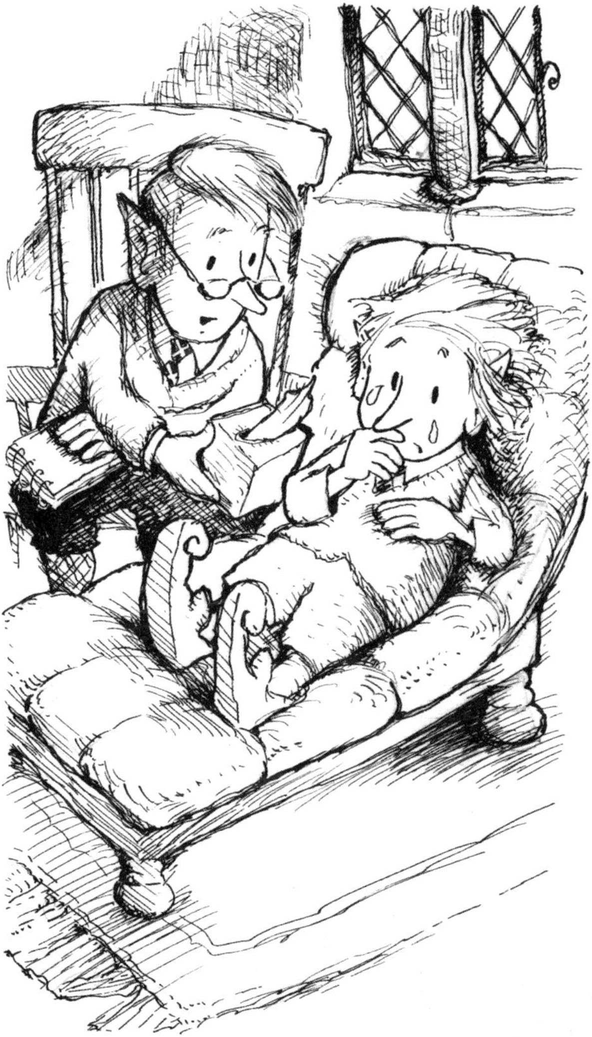

8.

Do you habitually run yourself down with thoughts like "It's my own fault..." or "If only I would have..."? Do you feel you are somehow defective or deficient because of your hurt? Work on overcoming this negative self-talk.

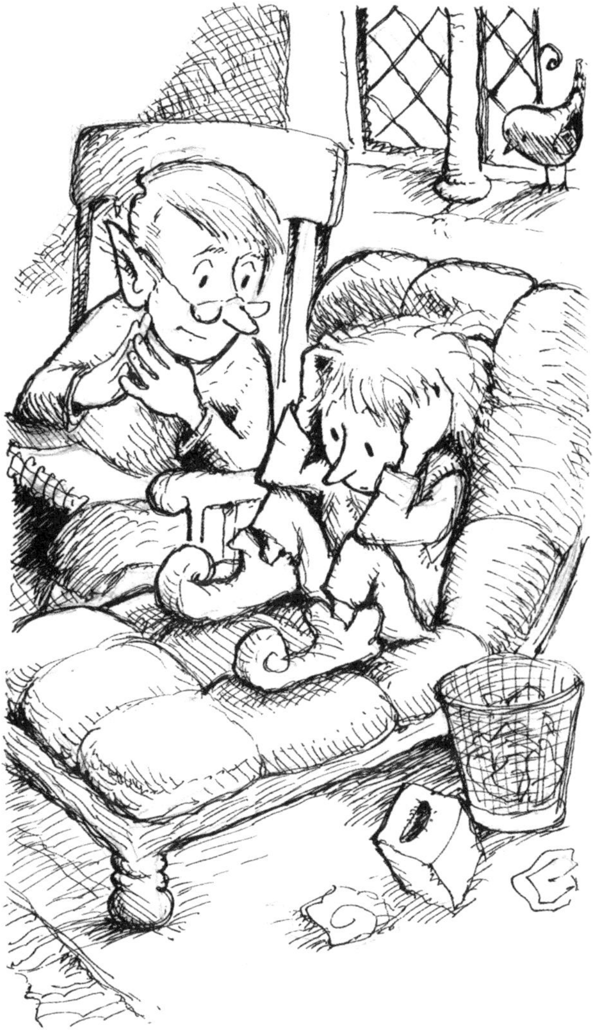

9.

God knows what you're going through and aches with you. God is on your side and in your heart—soothing, healing, empowering. Be alert to God helping you through the goodness of the people around you.

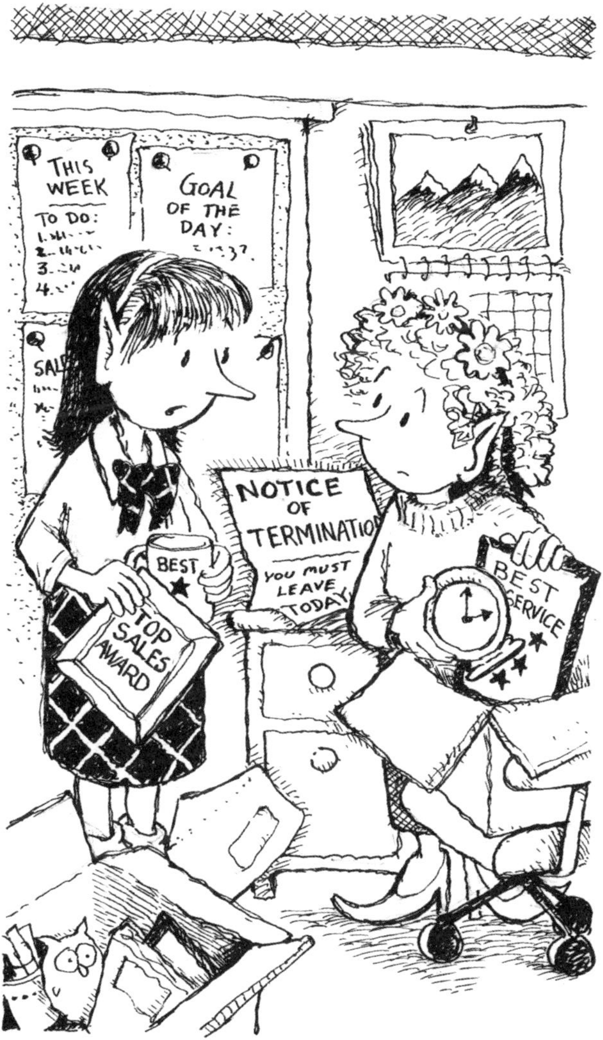
THIS WEEK
TO DO:
GOAL OF THE DAY:
NOTICE OF TERMINATIO
YOU MUST LEAVE TODAY
BEST
TOP SALES AWARD
BEST SERVICE

10.

Give physical expression to your crushed feelings. Cry, pummel your pillow, smack a racquetball. Do whatever helps you vent your emotions without harming yourself or others.

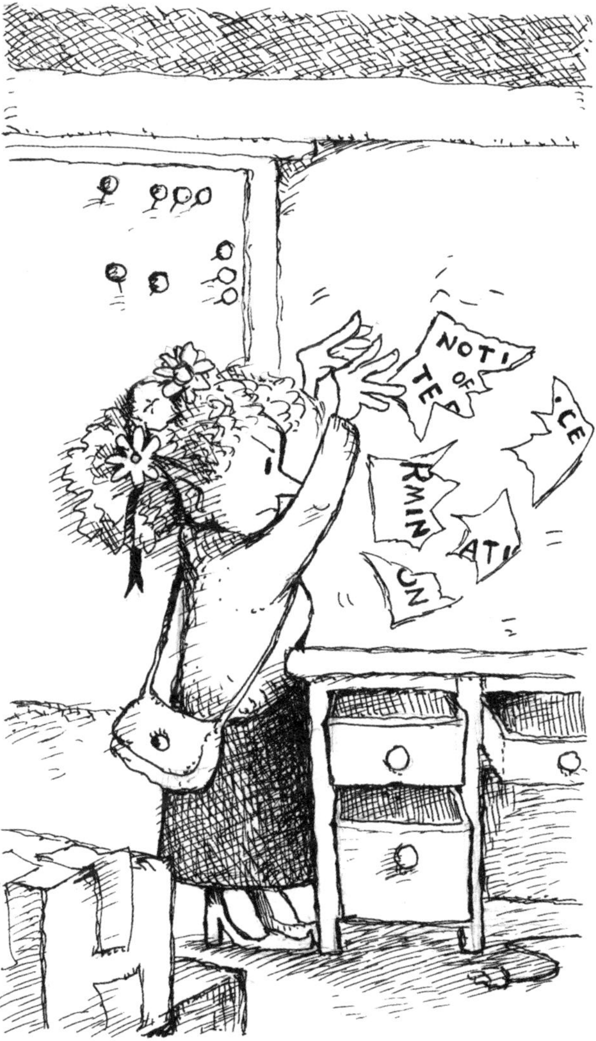
NOTI
OF
TE
CE
RMIN
ATI
ON

11.

With God all things are possible. Let God rekindle the light within your spirit and enfold you in tender mercy.

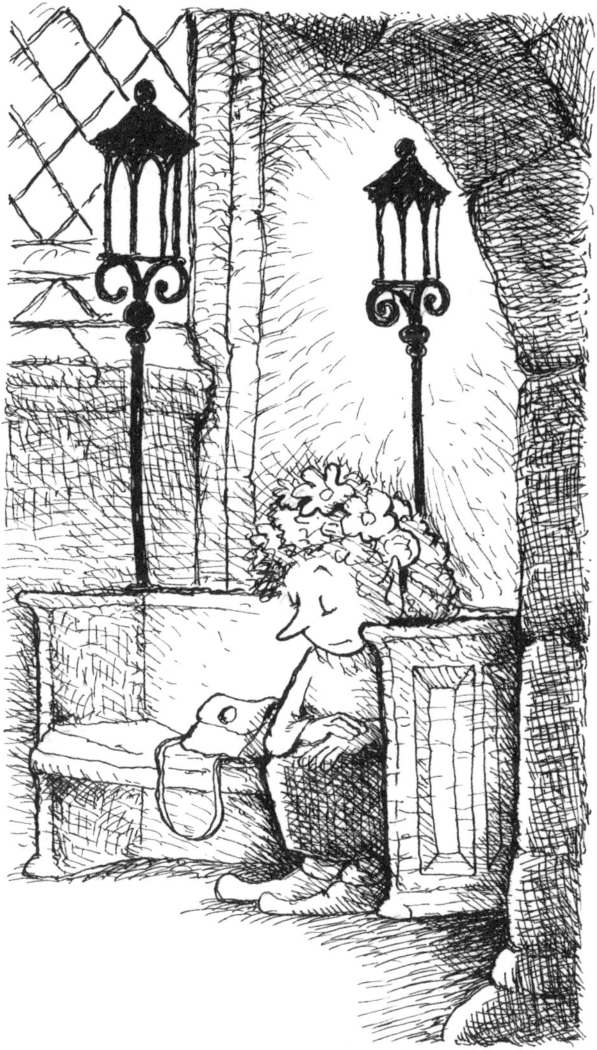

12.

When our prayers go
unanswered and God seems
far away, we can doubt faith
or want to rail against God.
Go ahead and rant.
God can take it.

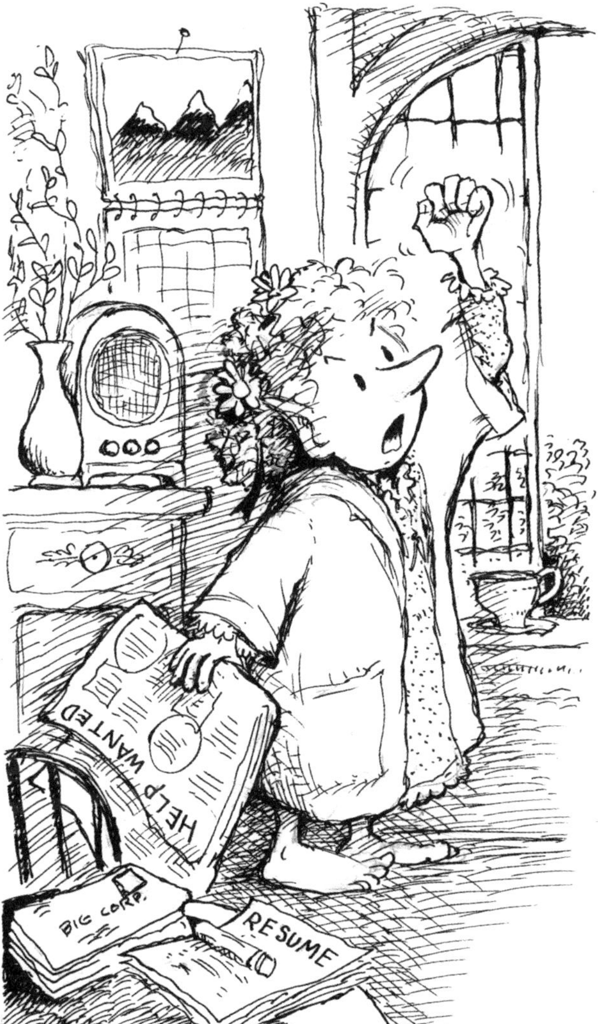
HELP WANTED
BIG CORP.
RESUME

13.

The hurt you feel today might actually date back to physical or emotional abuse you experienced long ago. Injuries like this can be so powerful they ripple through time and continue to damage your life.

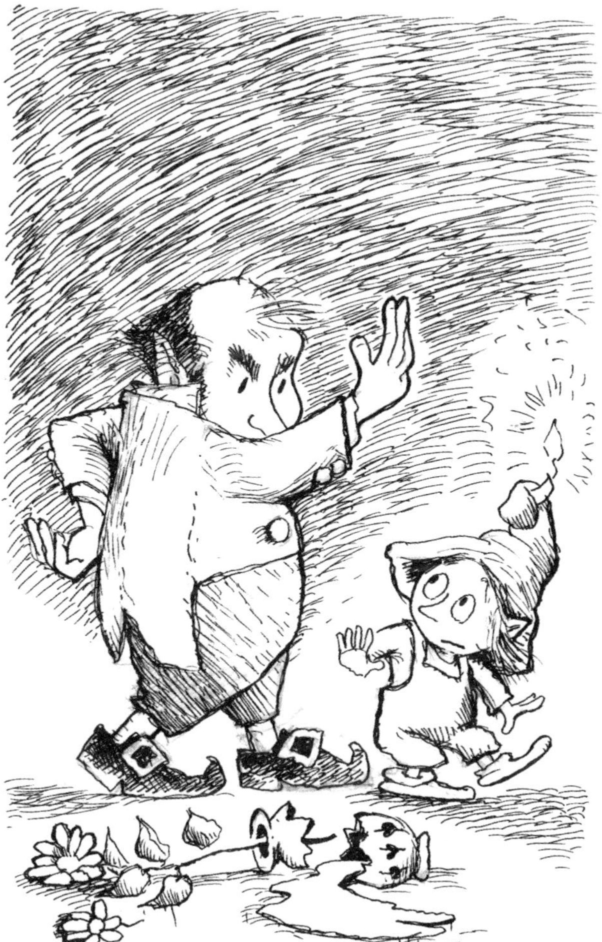

14.

Write a letter to the person who harmed you. You need not actually send it, but you may gain new insights into what happened, what you needed then, and what you need now.

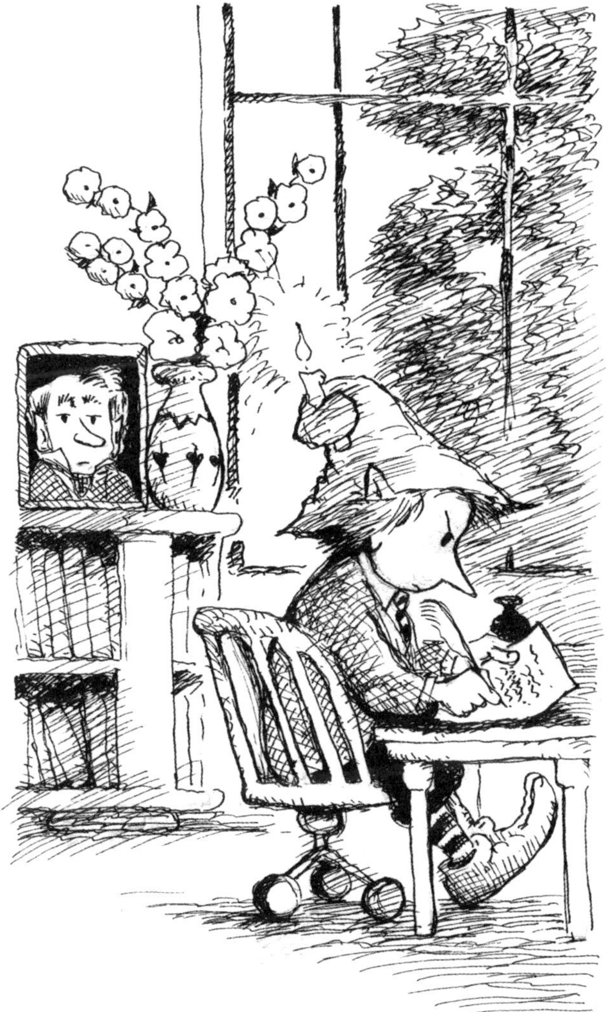

15.

If you must still have regular contact with this person who distresses you, try to limit your exposure. When you have to be together, put yourself in an imaginary "bubble," resistant to attacks or manipulation.

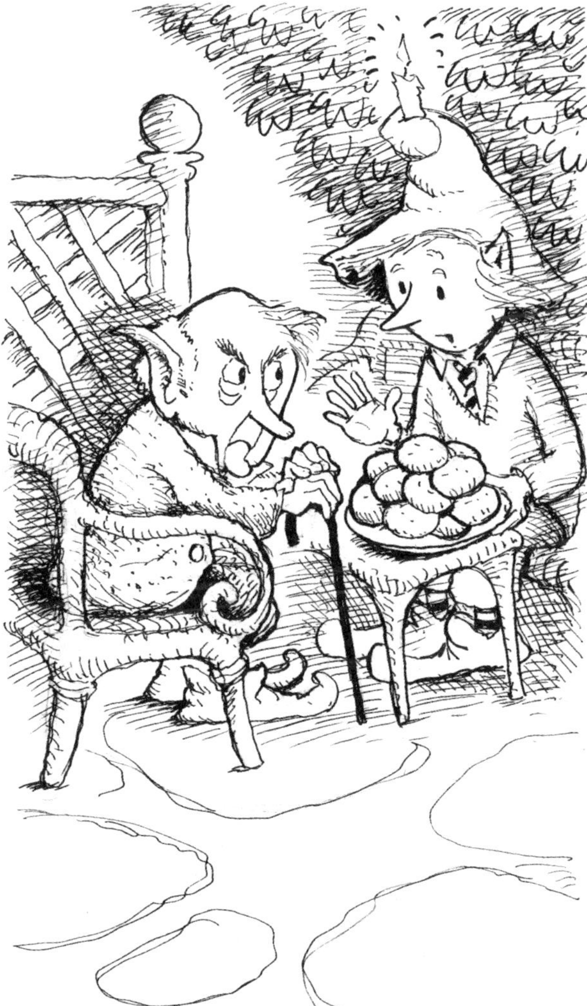

16.

If the emotional assault or insult is ongoing, you may need to confront your offender. Calmly state what is bothering you, why, and how it must end. You may not get an apology, but you will have stood up for yourself.

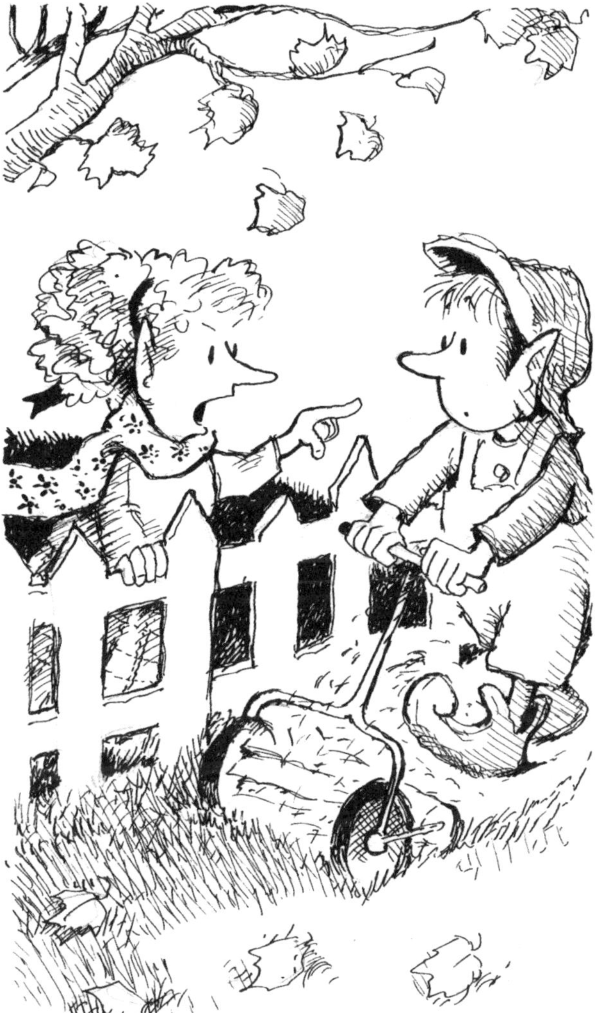

17.

Be open to the other person's perspective. You may find the offense was unintentional or get an apology. Or you might encounter denial and lack of remorse. If so, reevaluate whether this relationship is in your best interest.

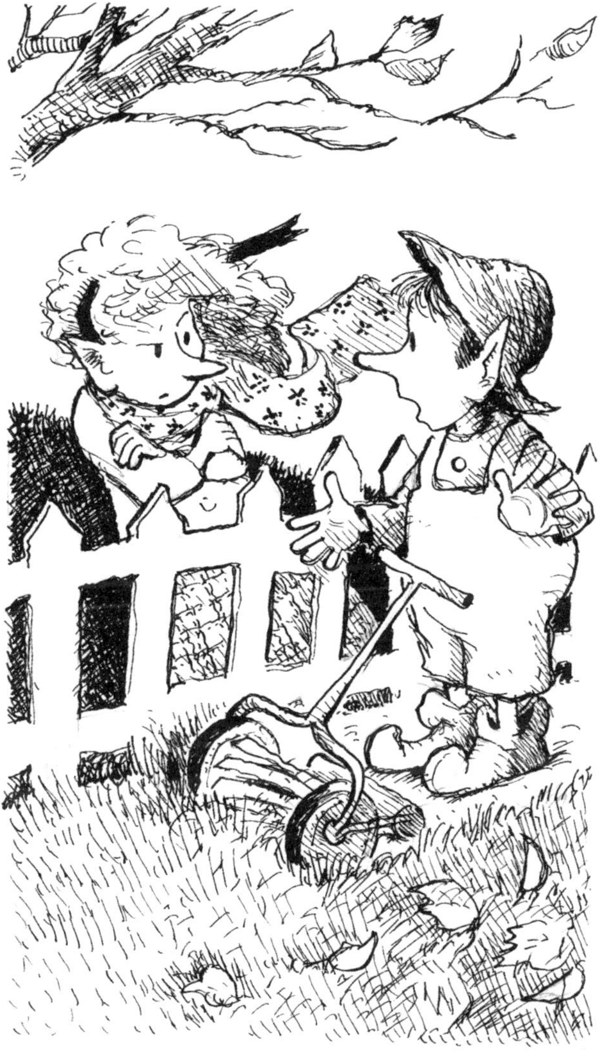

18.

We can sometimes become
hostile or oversensitive or
cynical to avoid further pain.
If this is the case, realize such
defenses are no longer serving
you well.

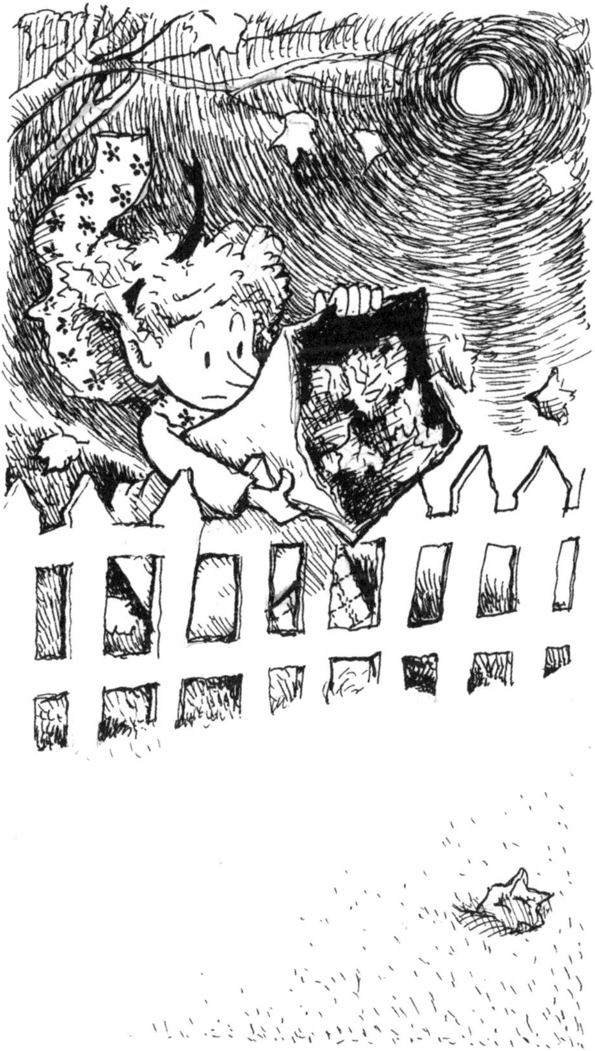

19.

People can be insensitive or downright mean. We can't change people, but we can choose our own reactions and attitudes.

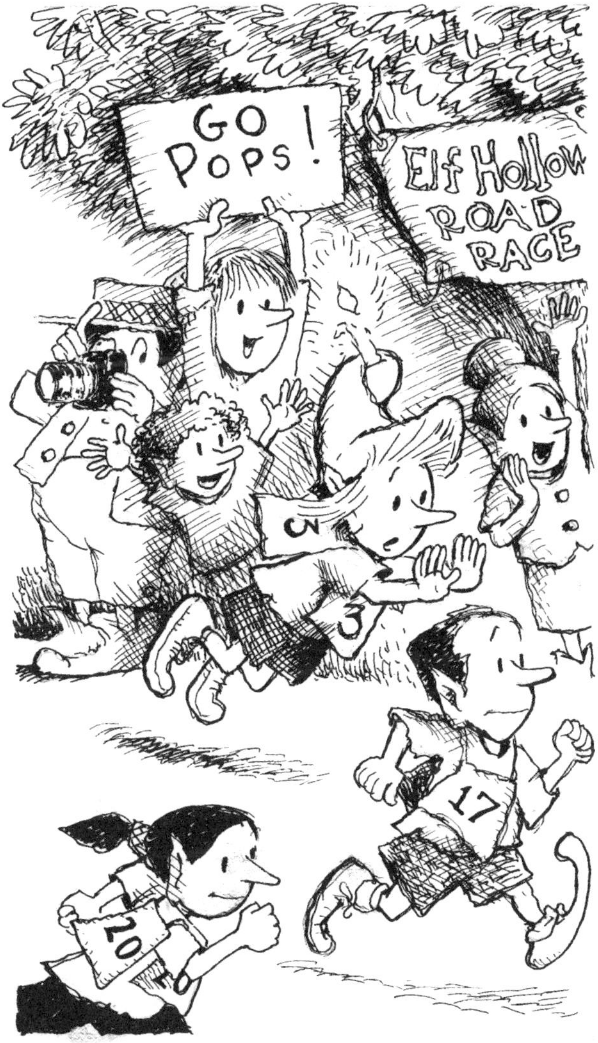
GO POPS!
Elf Hollow ROAD RACE
3
3
17
20

20.

We speak of "carrying" a grudge, and it is indeed a burden. If you're holding a grudge, consider whether it's worth the toll it's taking.

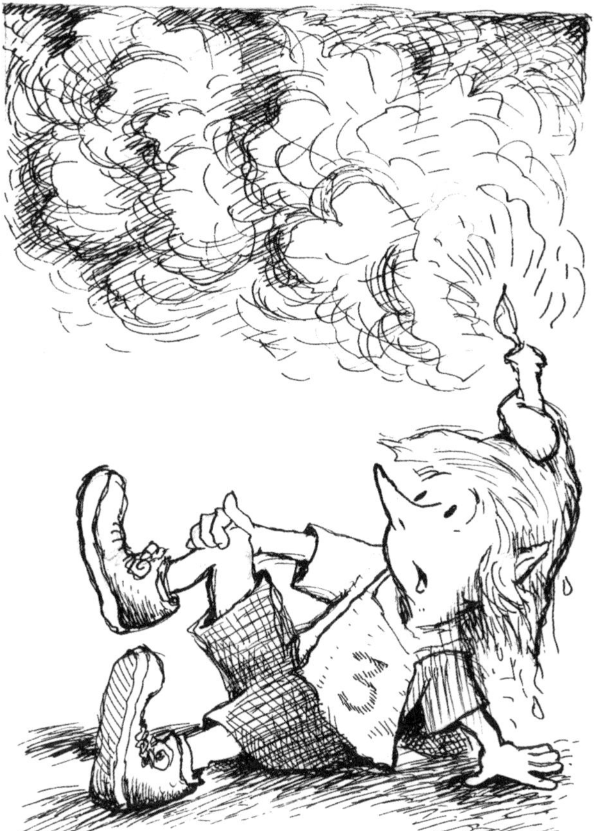

21.

The Buddha said: "Holding onto anger is like drinking poison and expecting the other person to die." Letting go of anger is something we do for our own good.

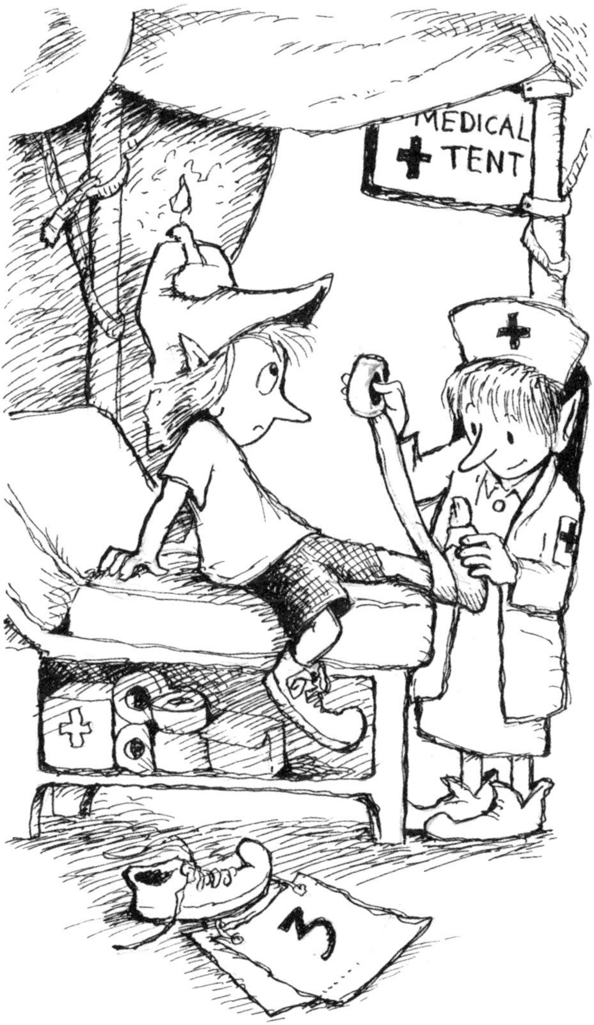
MEDICAL
TENT
3

22.

When we forgive, we don't have to do it by ourselves: "To err is human; to forgive is divine." Ask God for the power of forgiveness.

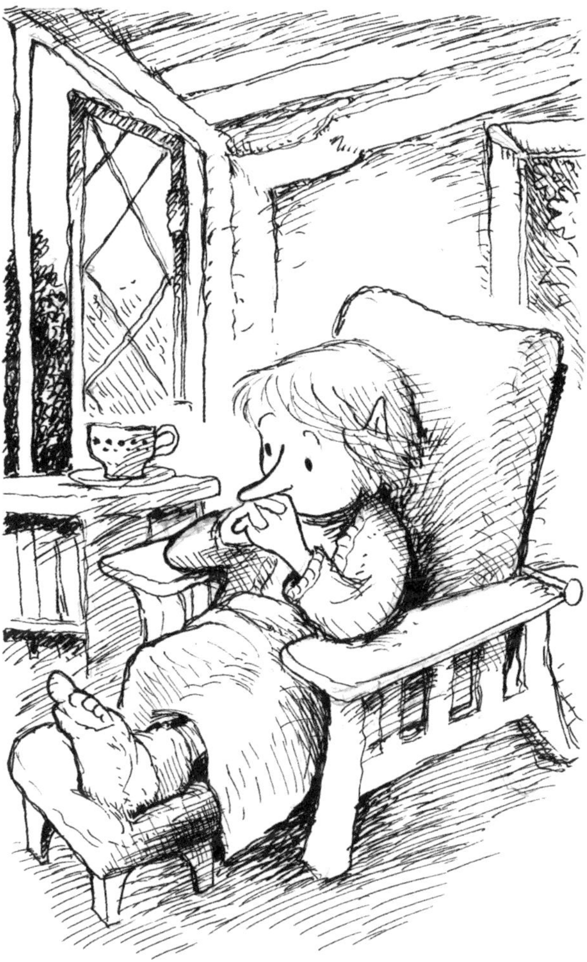

23.

We may need God's help to forgive again and again. Breathe out anger and resentment, so that you can fill up with God's love and light. Adopt a daily attitude of forgiveness.

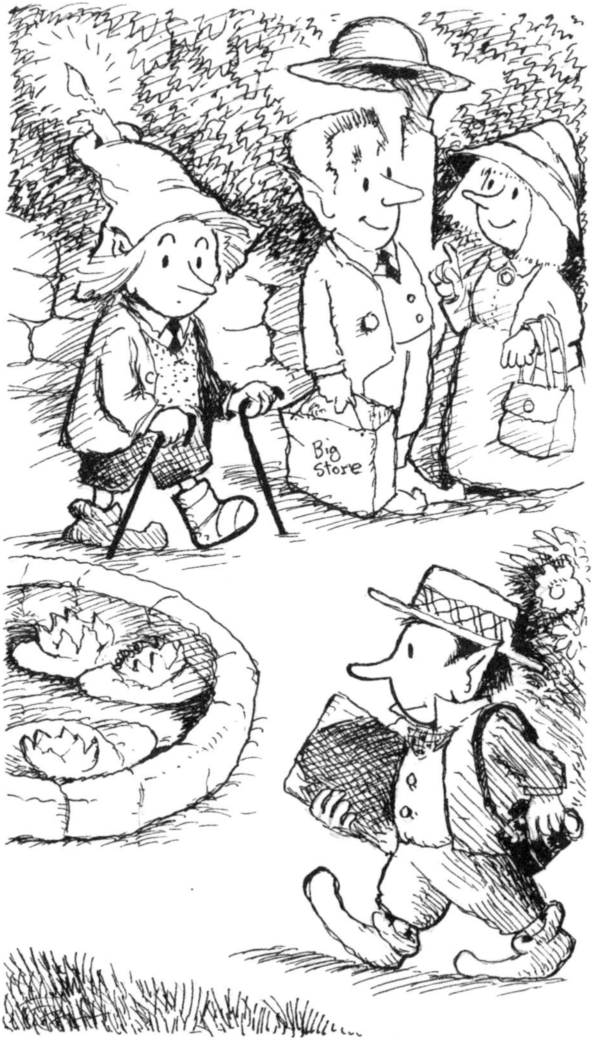
Big
Store

24.

The Bible has it right: Love your enemies. Pray for them. Wish them well—for their sake and your own. You will grow in understanding, compassion, and resilience.

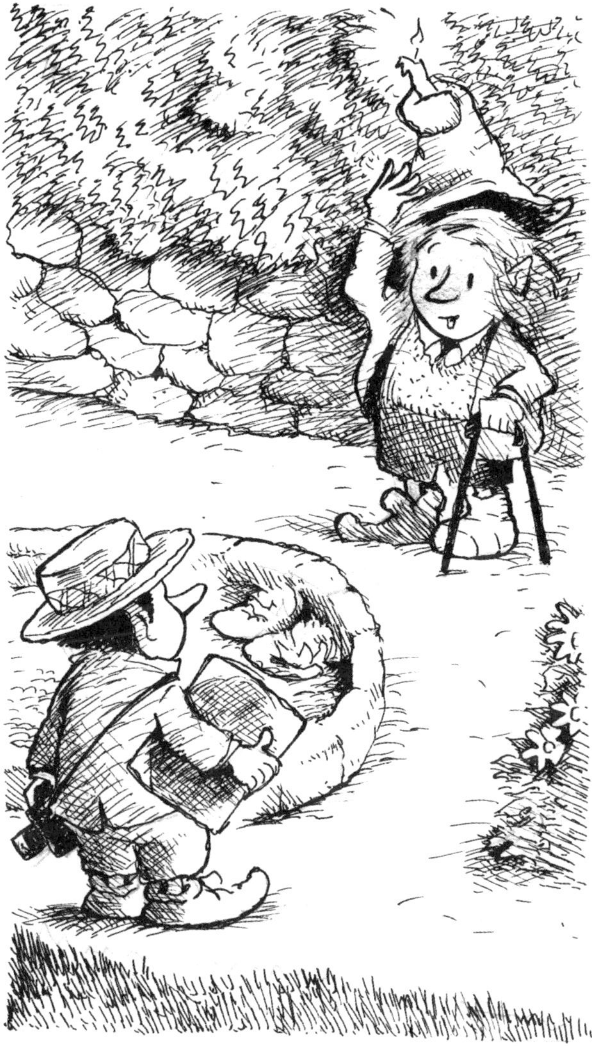

25.

Emotional stress can affect us physically. Consult with your doctor and take any needed steps to improve your physical wellbeing.

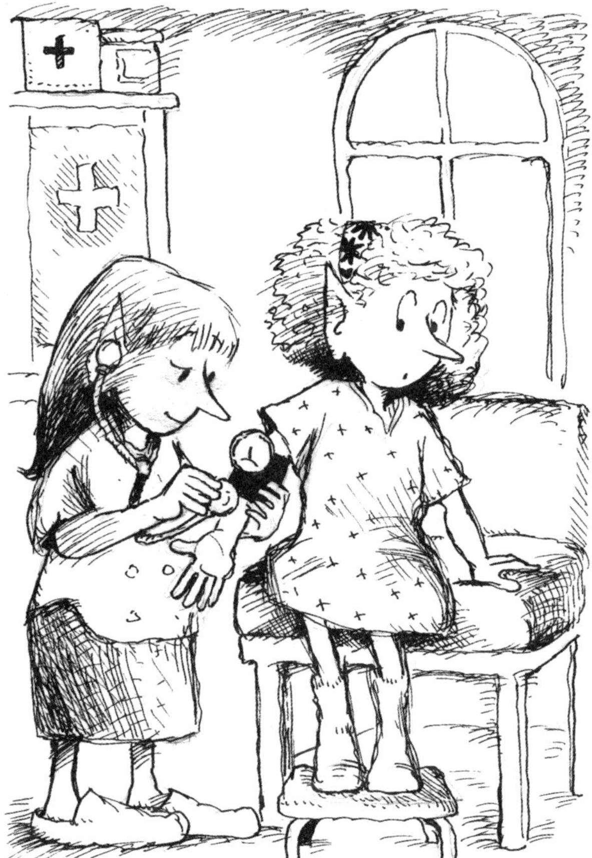

26.

Be kind to yourself. What
brings you pleasure and ease?
Let yourself find comfort in
whatever soothes your soul.

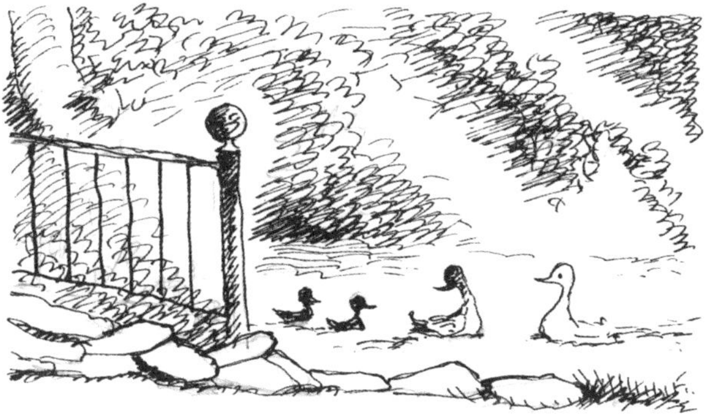

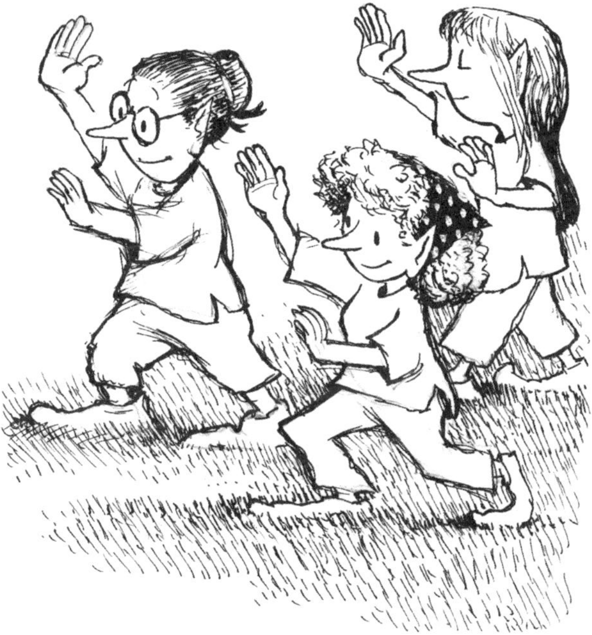

27.

While your wound is very personal, keeping it to yourself will only add to your sense of isolation. Confide in a friend, and you may be surprised to find true understanding.

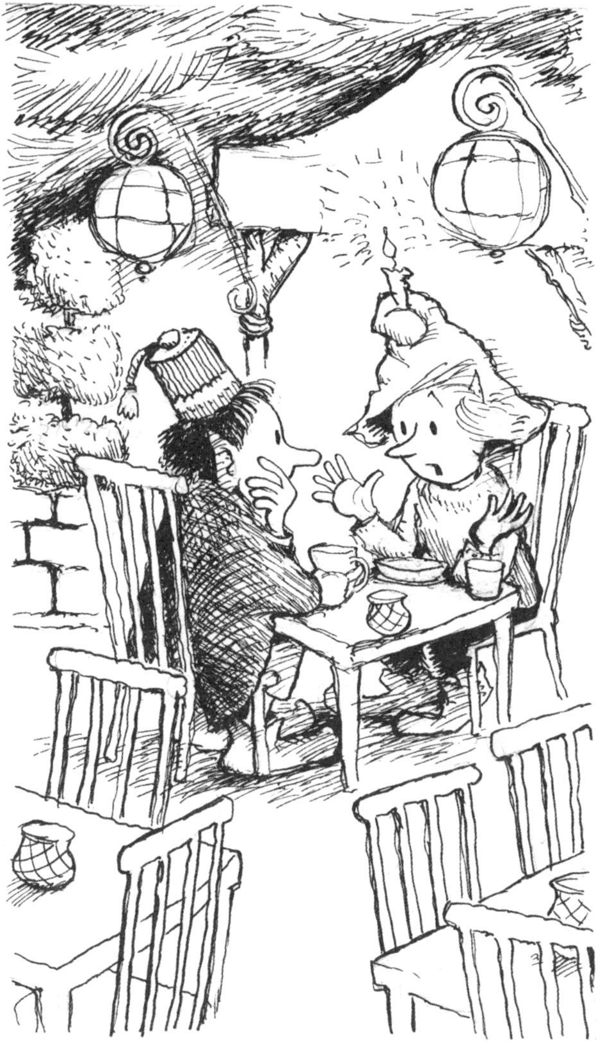

28.

Invest in yourself. You are worth it. Also consider alternative healing therapies, such as yoga, meditation, and acupuncture.

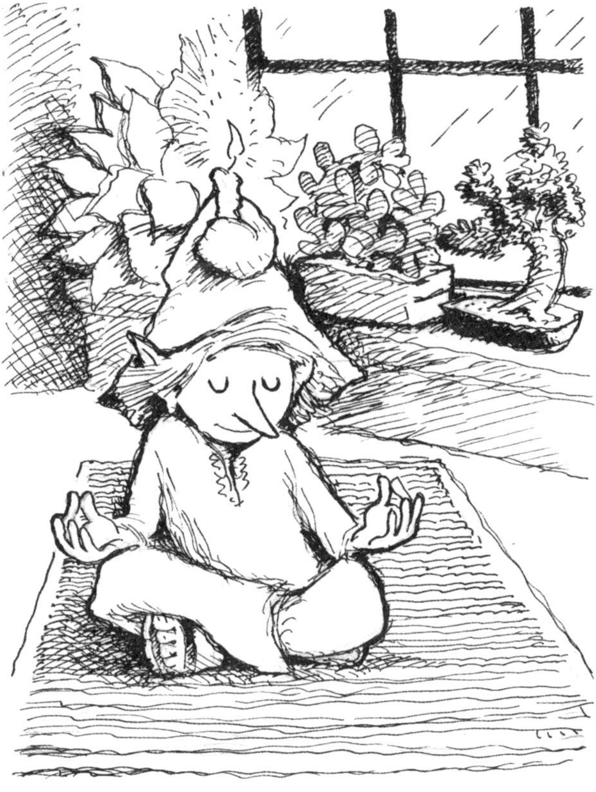

29.

In hindsight, you will see
how the seeds of healing were
sprouting before they were even
visible to you.

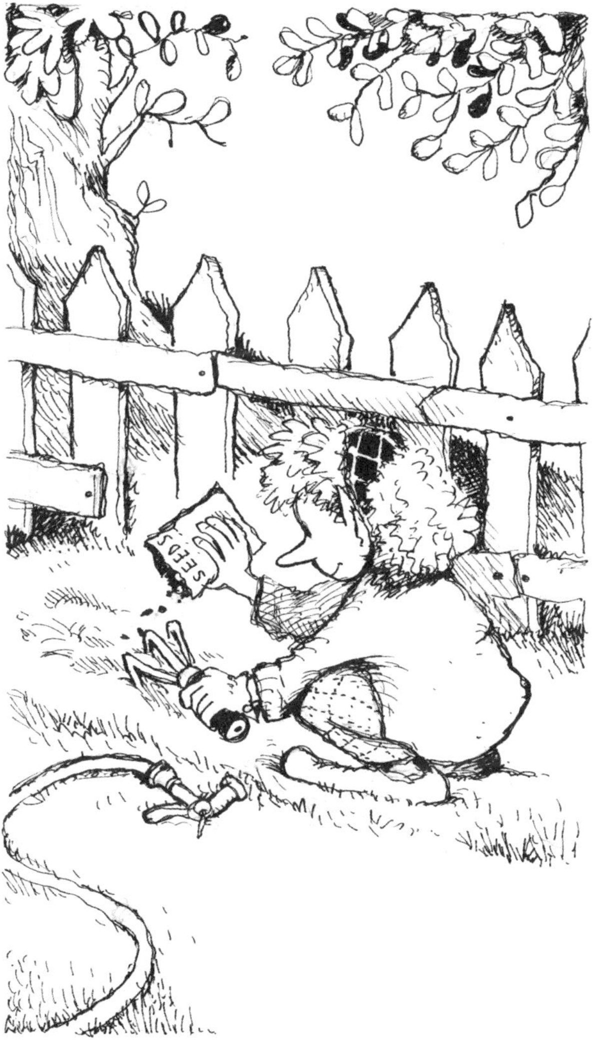
SEEDS

30.

Most miracles happen little by little. You look back months later and realize you are in a different, better place than you were before. You have moved on. You are healing.

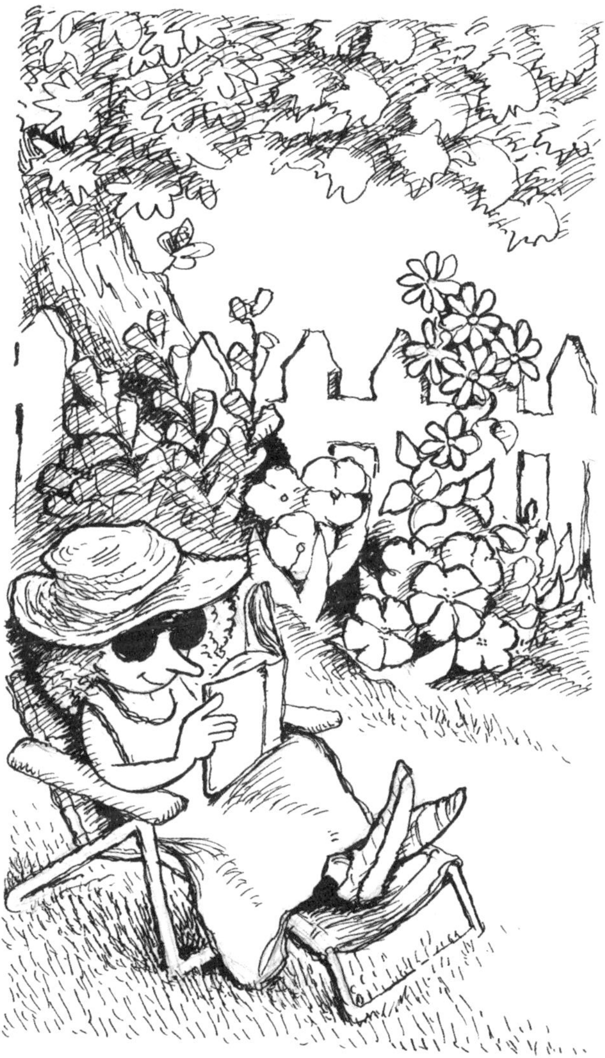

31.

Embrace the goodness of the universe: an unexpected kind word, a casserole from a neighbor, a baby's giggle. Savor life's bitty blessings and glimmers of grace.

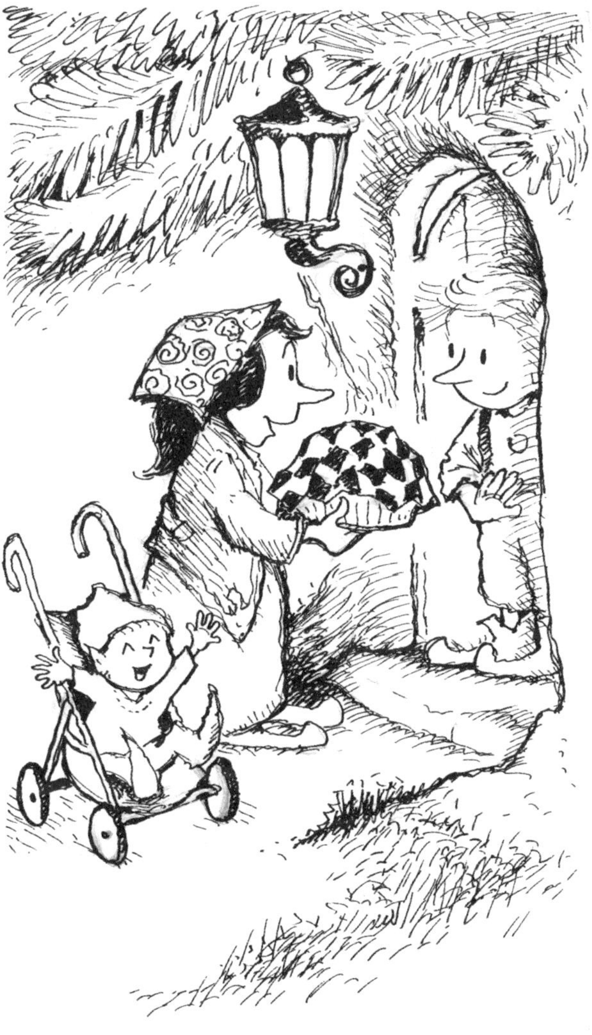

32.

Volunteer your time or other resources to a group that works to prevent or help heal the kind of suffering you experienced.

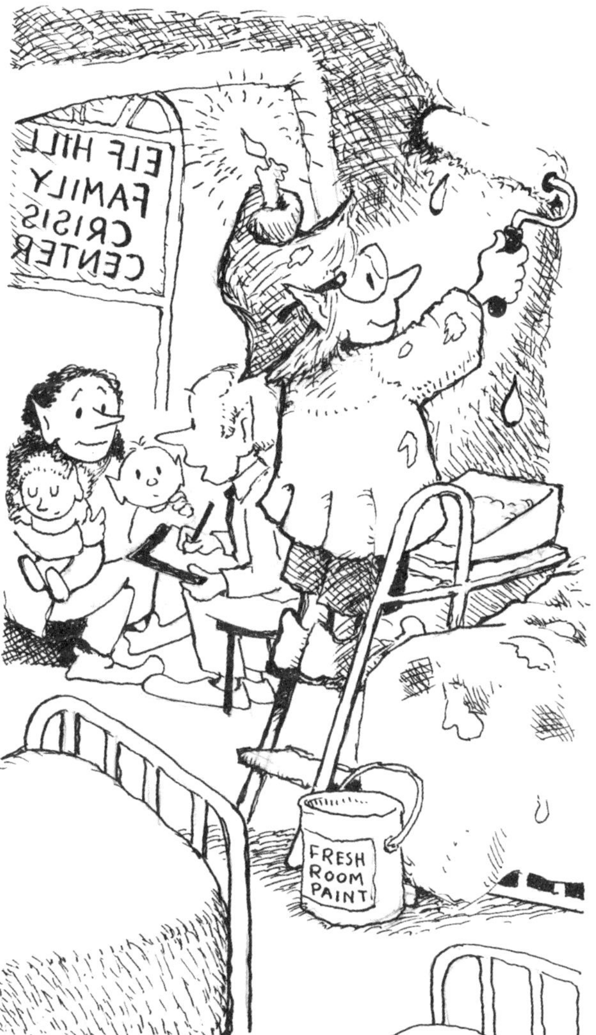
ELF HILL FAMILY CRISIS CENTER
FRESH ROOM PAINT

33.

Finding wholeness after hurt is a process. Like a physical injury, it takes time, patience, prayer, and persistence. Be grateful that you now know how to cope.

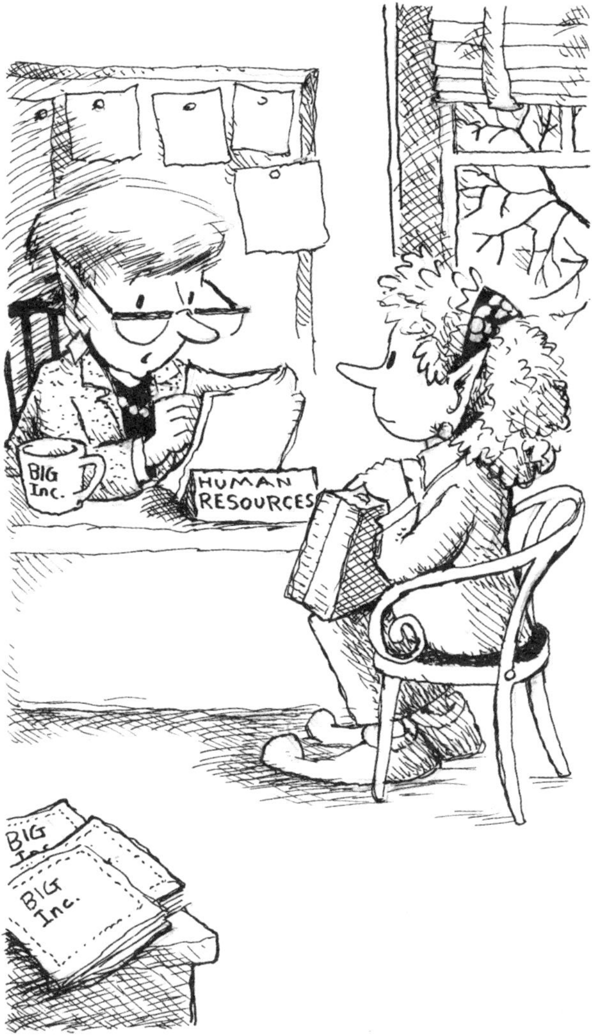
BIG Inc.
HUMAN RESOURCES
BIG Inc.

34.

You may feel very vulnerable on special anniversaries or with fresh reminders of your trauma. But you also now have the super-powers of self-knowledge, faith, forgiveness, and renewed strength.

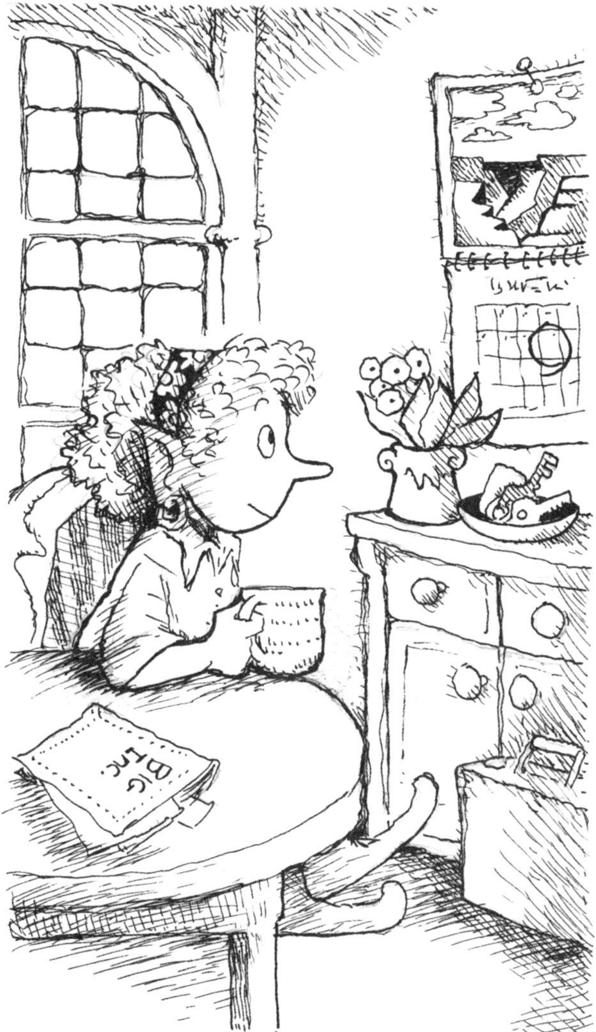

35.

See yourself as God sees you.
You are perfectly good, perfectly
formed to carry out your purpose
in the world.

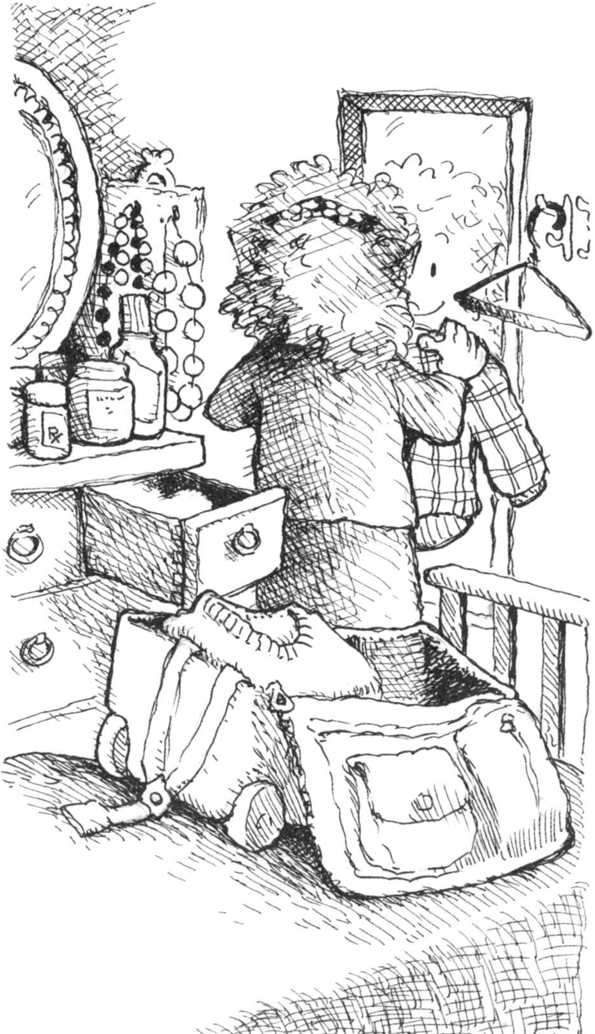

36.

"What hurts you, blesses you,"
the Persian poet Rumi wrote.
Like rock layers formed from
geologic pressure—true beauty
and strength can come from
great stress.

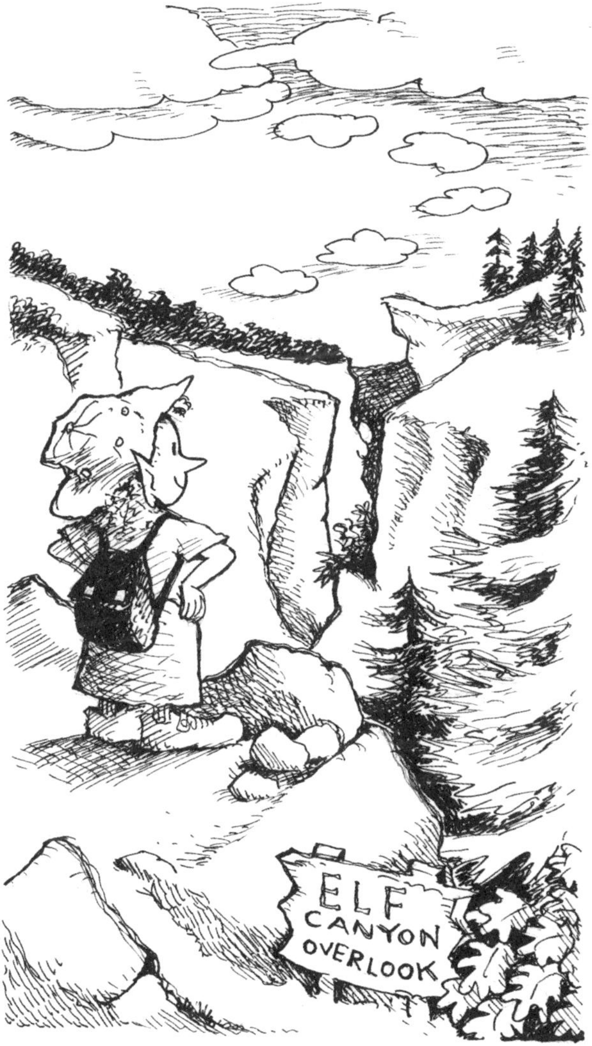
ELF
CANYON
OVERLOOK

37.

This ordeal is part of your character. You can let it shrivel your heart or you can let it show you the vast treasures of courage and wisdom your heart has to offer.

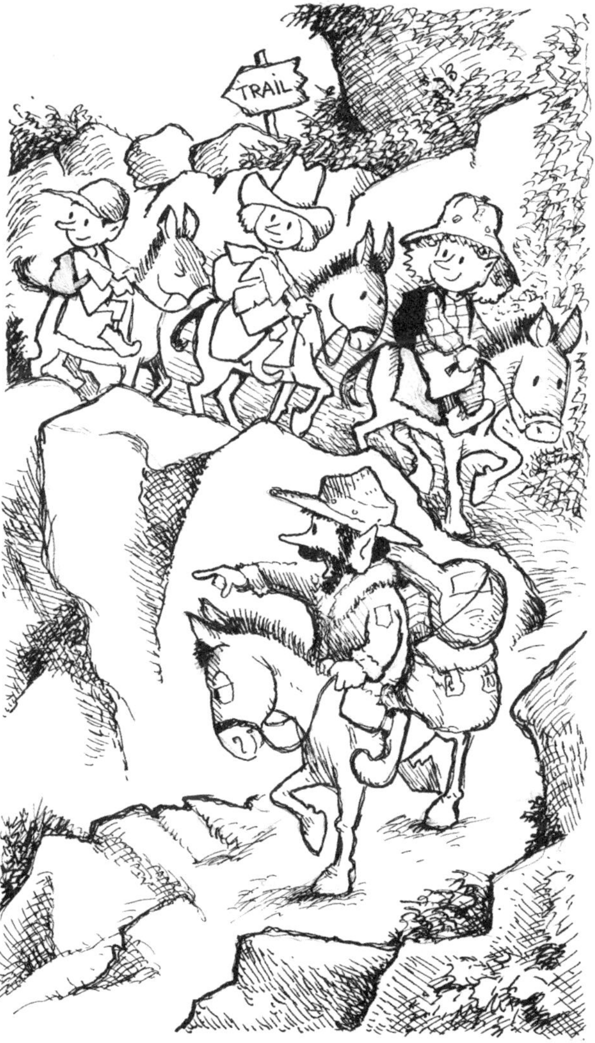
TRAIL

38.

You will never forget this hurt.
But you have learned from it
and grown from it. As you
harbor healing in your heart,
may you rediscover there deep
peace, love, and mercy.

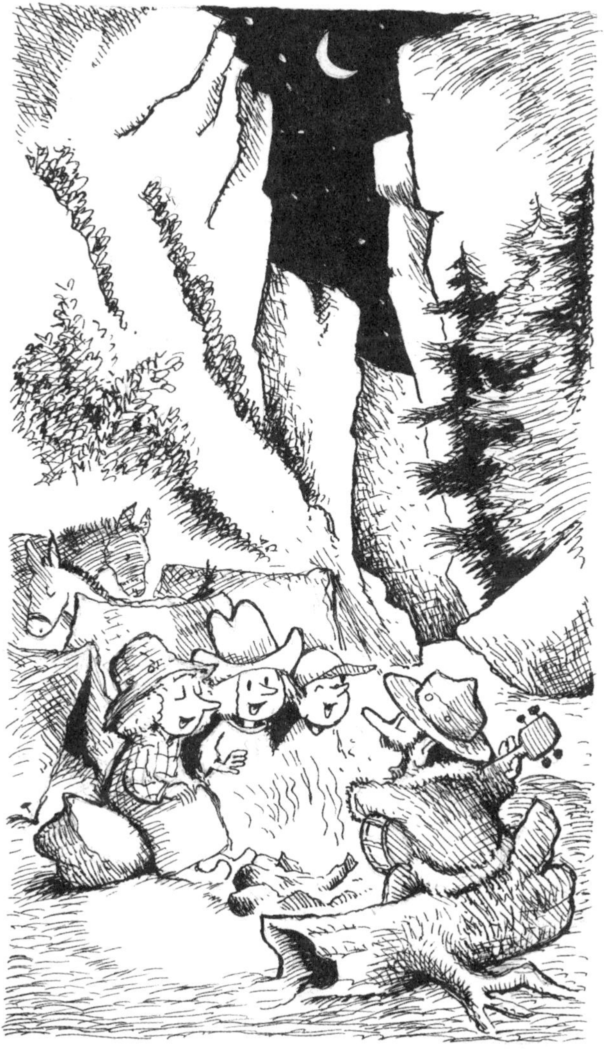

Lisa O. Engelhardt is a freelance writer who has authored 17 gift and children's books. A former editorial director for Abbey Press, she continues to write sentiments for greeting cards and giftware. She lives with her husband in Greater Cincinnati and enjoys yoga, reading, and humble attempts at painting.

Illustrator for the Abbey Press Elf-help Books, **R.W. Alley** also illustrates and writes children's books. He lives in Barrington, Rhode Island, with his wife, daughter, and son. See a wide variety of his works at: www.rwalley.com.

The Story of the Abbey Press Elves

The engaging figures that populate the Abbey Press "elf-help" line of publications and products first appeared in 1987 on the pages of a small self-help book called *Be-good-to-yourself Therapy*. Shaped by the publishing staff's vision and defined in R.W. Alley's inventive illustrations, they lived out author Cherry Hartman's gentle, self-nurturing advice with charm, poignancy, and humor.

Reader response was so enthusiastic that more Elf-help Books were soon under way, a still-growing series.

The especially endearing character featured in the early books—sporting a cap with a mood-changing candle in its peak—has since been joined by a spirited female elf with flowers in her hair.

These two exuberant, sensitive, resourceful, kindhearted, lovable sprites, along with their lively elfin community, reveal what's truly important as they offer messages of joy and wonder, playfulness and co-creation, wholeness and serenity, the miracle of life and the mystery of God's love.

With wisdom and whimsy, they demonstrate the elf-help way to a rich and fulfilling life.

Elf-help Books

...adding "a little character" and a lot
of help to self-help reading!

Elf-help for Coping With Pain	#20074
Elf-help for Dealing with Difficult People	#20076
Loneliness Therapy	#20078
'Tis a Blessing to Be Irish	#20088
Getting Older, Growing Wiser	#20089
Worry Therapy	#20093
Trust-in-God Therapy	#20119
Elf-help for Overcoming Depression	#20134
New Baby Therapy	#20140
Teacher Therapy	#20145
Stress Therapy	#20153
Get Well Therapy	#20157
Anger Therapy	#20127
Caregiver Therapy	#20164
Self-esteem Therapy	#20165
Peace Therapy	#20176
Friendship Therapy	#20174
Christmas Therapy (color edition)	#20175

Happy Birthday Therapy	#20181
Forgiveness Therapy	#20184
Keep-life-simple Therapy	#20185
Acceptance Therapy	#20190
Keeping-up-your-spirits Therapy	#20195
Slow-down Therapy	#20203
One-day-at-a-time Therapy	#20204
Prayer Therapy	#20206
Be-good-to-your-marriage Therapy	#20205
Be-good-to-yourself Therapy	#20255

Available at your favorite gift shop or bookstore—
or directly from Abbey Press Publications,
St. Meinrad, IN 47577.
Call 1-800-325-2511.
www.abbeypresspublications.com